Journal

Belongs to:

_____

_____

_____

Published by Better World Press, Inc.
A Division of Your True Nature, Inc.
P.O. Box 272309, Fort Collins, Colorado 80527
800-992-4769 email: branch@yourtruenature.com
yourtruenature.com

Silk painting cover and Illustrations: Ilan Shamir
Library of Congress Cataloging-in-Publication Data
ISBN: 9781930175389
    Shamir, Ilan, 1951-
        Advice from a Tree / Ilan Shamir
        1. Trees
        2. Human Growth and Potential
        3. Nature
        4. Health and Wellness

Printed in the USA on recycled paper. Many thanks to
the trees for their gift of paper! All paper used in the printing of this
book has been replanted through the 100% Replanted program.
Visit www.ReplantTrees.org.

Suggestions for using the
Advice from a Tree Journal

Nature is a timeless and magnificent guide to help us in simple, thoughtful ways. Through the beauty of the trees, we can remember and reconnect with the joys of life, growth, and personal achievement, as well as with our own health and well being.

Trees are an amazing gift!
They are great teachers simply by reflecting and living their true nature. An oak is proud to be a beautiful oak—it doesn't spend energy trying to be an aspen. In simple ways, trees remind us to be the beauty of ourselves!

Often, as we remember our favorite tree or tree experience, wonderful feelings and memories arise within us. The experience of reconnecting with our roots can help us live our highest and truest nature. You may want to journal about your tree experiences or other gardening, hiking, or walking in nature experiences.

Sixteen of the journal pages have a line from the "Advice from a Tree" poem. On the "Stand tall and proud" page, and the blank pages that follow, you might make notes about ways that you feel good about yourself or ideas for how you might stand taller and prouder. The "Think long term" pages invite you to list your goals and aspirations and steps in achieving them. For the "Drink plenty of water" pages, record your thoughts about ways to nurture your strength and health.

Use the pages of this tree journal however you like. You may want to use it as a way to harmonize your own cycles and seasons with those of nature. Write, draw, paste your favorite pictures . . . most of all, have fun!

I think I'll "leaf" you to the joys and discoveries of your journaling. And never forget . . . you're tree-mendous!

Inspired by a Tree . . .

It was one of those difficult days . . .
one of those days that tore at the very roots of my
being. I just had to get outside to breathe and somehow
find a way back to my center, to return to the peace and
clarity of my soul. I managed to open the front door
and, with tears in my eyes, I began to move along the
sidewalk, lifting one foot in front of the other without
a clue where I was going. Exhausted, I leaned against
a huge cottonwood tree; the deep ridges of the bark
held me close. I said, "I've been working for you for many
years now, planting thousands of trees, teaching about
the miracles of the earth. Now I need your help! Can you
help me? I need some advice." I felt the tree reach out to
me, wrap me in its branches, and comfort me as I leaned
against its steady trunk. This old and wise cottonwood
tree spoke to me with clarity and wisdom. I felt hopeful,
renewed, and loved, and went home and I wrote the
following caring message from this tree friend . . . .

Ilan Shamir

Advice from a Tree

Dear Friend . . .
Stand tall and proud
Sink your roots deep into the earth
Reflect the light of your true nature
Think long-term
Go out on a limb

Remember your place among all living beings
Embrace with joy the changing seasons,
for each yields its own abundance:
The energy and birth of spring
The growth and contentment of summer

The wisdom to let go like leaves in the fall
The rest and quiet renewal of winter

Feel the wind and the sun
And delight in their presence
Look up at the moon that shines down upon you
And the mystery of the stars at night
Seek nourishment from the good things in life
Simple pleasures . . .
Earth, fresh air, light

Be content with your natural beauty
Drink plenty of water
Let your limbs sway and dance in the breezes
Be flexible
Remember your roots

Enjoy the view!

Dear Friend . . .

Stand tall and proud!

Sink your roots
         deep into the earth

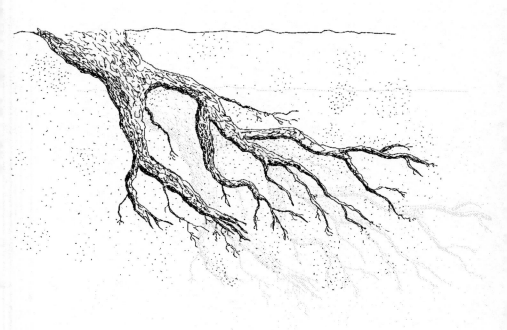

Reflect the light
of your own true nature

Once a very old man
was planting trees.
A young girl came up to him and said,
"Why are you planting trees?
You will never be around
to see them mature."
His reply was simple,
"I do not plant them for myself—
I plant them for future generations!"
. . . As a child, he had so much
enjoyed the magnificience
of the trees that had been planted
years before that he wanted
to show his appreciation
and give the earth
his own special gift.

Think
l o n g
term

Go out on a limb

Remember your place
among all living beings

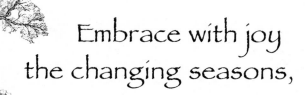

Embrace with joy
the changing seasons,

for each yields its own abundance:

The energy and birth of spring

The growth and contentment
of summer

The wisdom to let go
like leaves in the fall

The rest and quiet renewal of winter

Feel the wind and the sun
And delight in their presence
Look up at the moon that shines down upon you
And the mystery of the stars at night
Seek nourishment from the good things in life
Simple pleasures . . .
Earth, fresh air, light

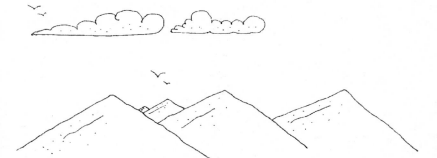

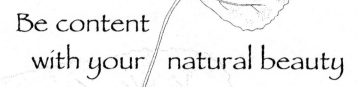

Be content
with your natural beauty

Drink plenty of water

Let your limbs sway and dance
in the breezes

Be flexible

Remember your roots

Enjoy the view!

Ilan Shamir's
Advice Book Series

 Advice from a Tree &
Accompanying Journal

 Advice from a River &
Accompanying Journal

 Advice from a Mountain &
Accompanying Journal

 Advice from a Garden

Advice from Nature
 (Includes Advice from a Sea Turtle,
Owl, Canyon and many more)

More Advice from Nature
(Includes Advice from a Moose,
Wildflower, Night Sky and many more)

Other Titles

Tree Celebrations-
Planting and Celebrating Trees

PoetTree-
The Wilderness I Am

Simple Wisdom-
A Thousand Things Went Right Today!

The True Nature of Designing and
Promoting Successful Products

The True Nature of Designing and
Promoting Successful Programs

My Colorado
Nuggets of Wit and Wisdom

Words

We invite you to visit us at:
yourtruenature.com for hundreds of other
items including collectable frameable art
cards, bookmarks, posters, mugs, magnets,
t-shirts and more.

* Keynote programs
* Breakouts
* Workshops

Through the simplicity and beauty of trees and nature, Ilan Shamir calls us to branch out, grow, and celebrate our true nature! Author of the bestselling Advice from a Tree products and "A Thousand Things Went Right Today," Ilan's inspiring programs are a perfect addition to conferences and events.

Member of the:
*National Associaton for Interpretation
*National Speakers Association Colorado
*National Storytellers Network

yourtruenature.com

Have a Tree Planted for Someone Special!

Your purchase price of $8.95 for one tree, or $18.95 for a three-tree grove, plants and cares for native trees in projects in El Salvador, Honduras, Costa Rica, and Nicaragua through the nonprofit organization Trees, Water & People. The recipient gets a beautiful personalized greeting card from you, and both you and the recipient can visit the planting area online!

A simple gift that lasts a lifetime!
It's as easy as 1, 2, TREE . . .

Qty ($8.95)	Qty ($18.95)	Occasion
___	___	**All Occasion**

(Friendship, birthday, Mother's Day, thank you, birth, anniversary, congratulations, Father's Day, wedding, graduation)

___	Holiday
___	Memorial

Your Name _____
Address _____
City/State/ZIP _____
Email _____
Telephone _____

Total Qty _____ at $ 8.95 = $_____
Total Qty _____ at $18.95 = $_____
Shipping $_____6.50
GRAND TOTAL $_____

Send with your check to:
Your True Nature, Inc. Box 272309
Fort Collins, CO 80527, (970)282-1620
Email: orders@yourtruenature.com
Visit our website for more information or to order online at yourtruenature.com

When you plant a tree,
You grow a friend.
A friend you'll have for life.

Ilan Shamir & Sheldon Sands